阿祁的涂色旅行
Aki's Colouring Travel Book

这里是**上海**
This is Shanghai

黄瑶瑶 绘

中国城市出版社
CHINA CITY PRESS

那行 策划/出品

简介 Introduction

上海是我们国家的直辖市，简称"沪"，位于中国华东地区，地处长江入海口，东隔东中国海与日本九州岛相邻，南濒杭州湾。上海是中国的经济、金融、贸易、航运、科技创新中心。

小朋友来过上海吗？那你知道外滩边上的江叫什么名字吗？知道中国第一高楼是哪一栋吗？人民广场以前的名字叫什么吗？……

如果现在还不知道，也没关系哦。在这本填色书里有一只叫阿姬的猫咪，她会带着你一起游玩上海，和阿姬一起开心地去逛吧～要知道，阿姬不仅是一只旅行喵哦，她也是一只贪吃喵。为什么这么说呢？小朋友往下翻就会知道啦！

Shanghai is a municipality under the direct administration of central government, referred as "Hu" for short. Located in East China, it is at the mouth of the Yangtze River, east of the East China Sea and Kyushu Island in Japan, and south of Hangzhou Bay. Shanghai is the center for economic, financial, trading, shipping, technology innovation in China.

Have you even been to Shanghai? Do you know the name of the river by the Bund? Do you know which building is the tallest high-rise in China? What was the former name for People's Square?

No worries if you have no idea. In this coloring book, there is a cat named Aki, who will take you to a delightful journey in Shanghai. You know what? Aki is not only a wanderer, but also a gourmet. And why? Just turn over the page!

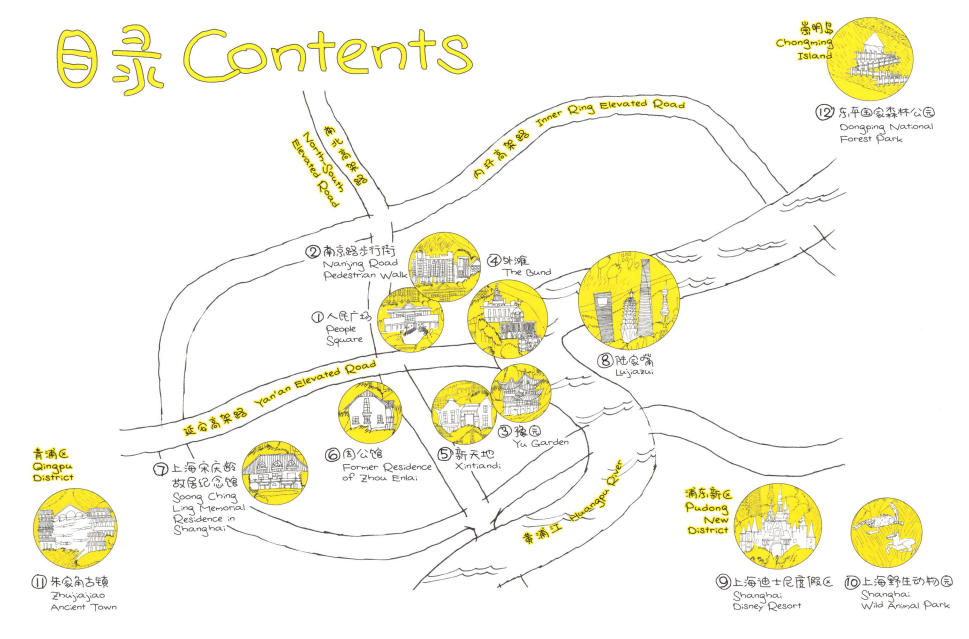

① 人民广场 People Square

Q：人民广场以前的名称叫什么？

大家对人民广场再熟悉不过了吧？人民广场原来叫作上海跑马厅，是当时上海名流们举行赛马等活动的场所。而现在的人民广场是一个开放式的广场，可以容纳120多万人。这里有上海博物馆、上海历史博物馆、上海城市规划馆，还有上海大剧院哦！

开放时间：全天

Q: What was People's Square called in the past?
I bet you couldn't be more familiar with People's Square! Originally known as the Shanghai Race Hall, it was once the place where celebrities held horse racing and other activities. Now People's Square is an open square that can accommodate more than 1.2 million people. You can also find Shanghai Museum, Shanghai History Museum, Shanghai Urban Planning Exhibition Center and Shanghai Grand Theater here!

Opening hours: All day

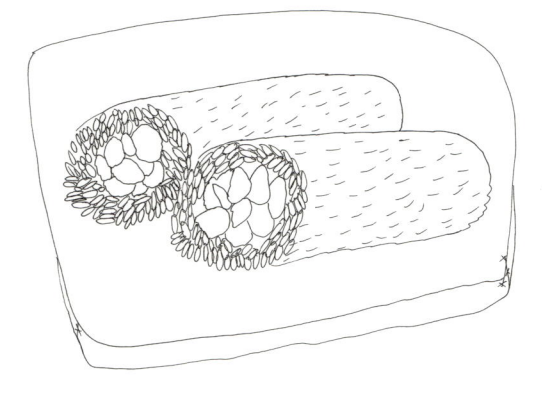

粢饭团
Glutinous Rice Balls

-4-

南京路步行街
Nanjing Road Pedestrian Walk

Q：小朋友们知道很长很长的南京路步行街到底有多长吗？

南京路步行街全长有1033米，采用不对称的布置形式，是一条有4.2米宽的"金带"。"金带"上集中布置了各种城市公共设施，比如座椅、购物亭、问讯亭、广告牌等等，而且还有34个造型各异的花坛。

开放时间：全天

Q: Guess the length of this super long Nanjing Road pedestrian walk?
Nanjing Road Pedestrian Walk is 1,033 meters long and follows an asymmetrical layout. It is a 4.2-meter-wide "Golden Belt", equipped with various urban public facilities such as benches, vending machines, kiosks, billboards, etc, and 34 flower beds in different shapes.
Opening hours: All day

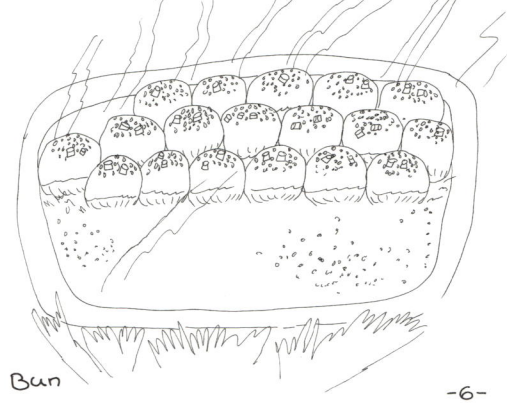

生煎包
Pan-Fried Bun

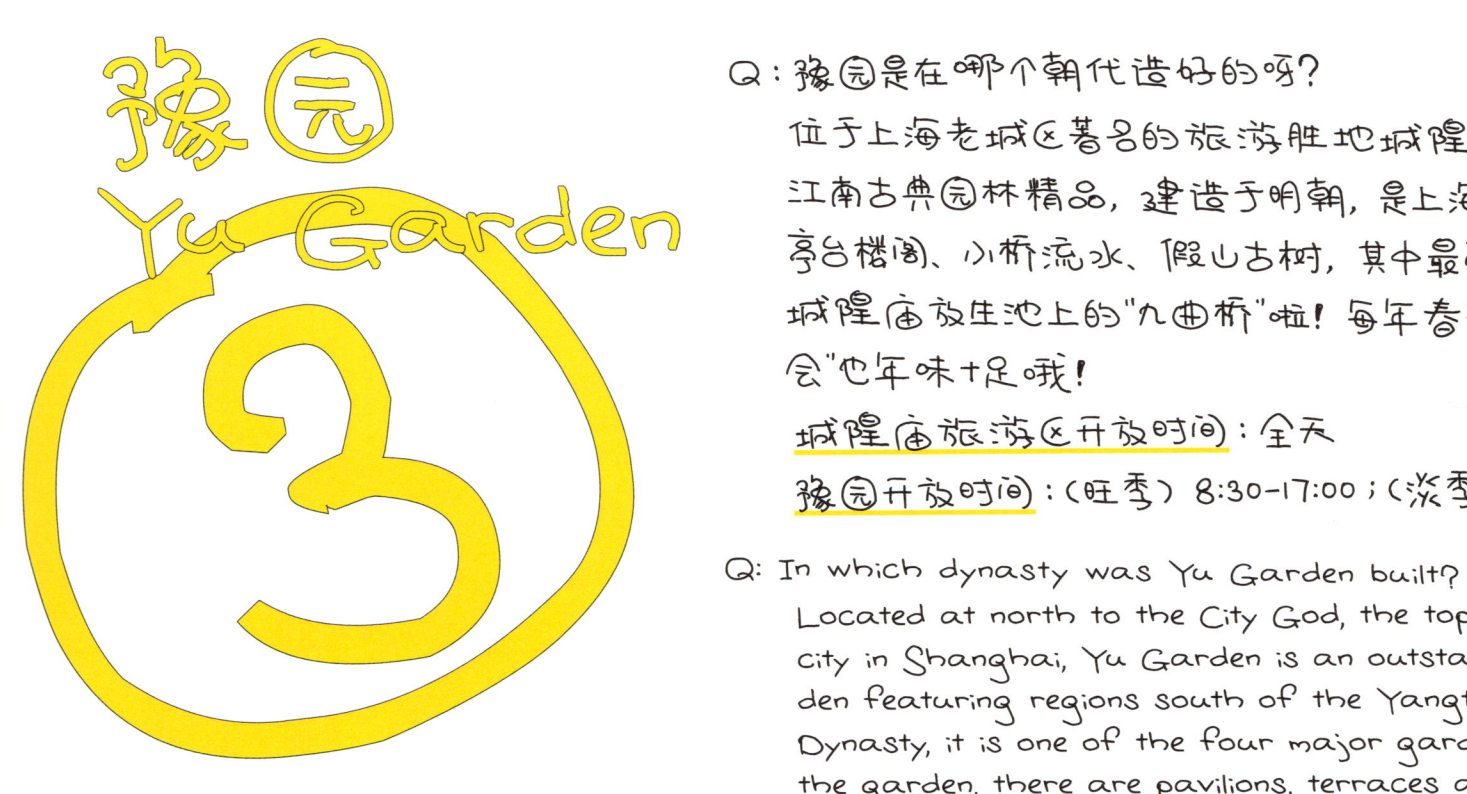

豫园
Yu Garden
③

小笼包
Steamed
Bunk

Q：豫园是在哪个朝代造好的呀？

位于上海老城区著名的旅游胜地城隍庙北侧的豫园是一座江南古典园林精品，建造于明朝，是上海四大园林之一。园内有亭台楼阁、小桥流水、假山古树，其中最受小朋友欢迎的就是城隍庙放生池上的"九曲桥"啦！每年春节的"豫园民俗艺术灯会"也年味十足哦！

城隍庙旅游区开放时间：全天

豫园开放时间：（旺季）8:30-17:00；（淡季）8:30-16:30

Q: In which dynasty was Yu Garden built?

Located at north to the City God, the top attraction of the old city in Shanghai, Yu Garden is an outstanding classical garden featuring regions south of the Yangtze River. Built in Ming Dynasty, it is one of the four major gardens in Shanghai. In the garden, there are pavilions, terraces and open halls, small bridges over the flowing stream, rockeries and ancient trees. The most popular one among children is the "Zigzag Bridge" (namely a bridge which makes nine turns) above the Free Life Pond. The annual "Yu Garden Lantern Festival" certainly adds more traditional joyous atmosphere to Chinese New Year!

Opening hours of Town God's Temple tourist area: All day
Yu Garden Opening hours:
(peak season) 8:30-17:00; (off-peak season) 8:30-16:30

外滩 The Bund

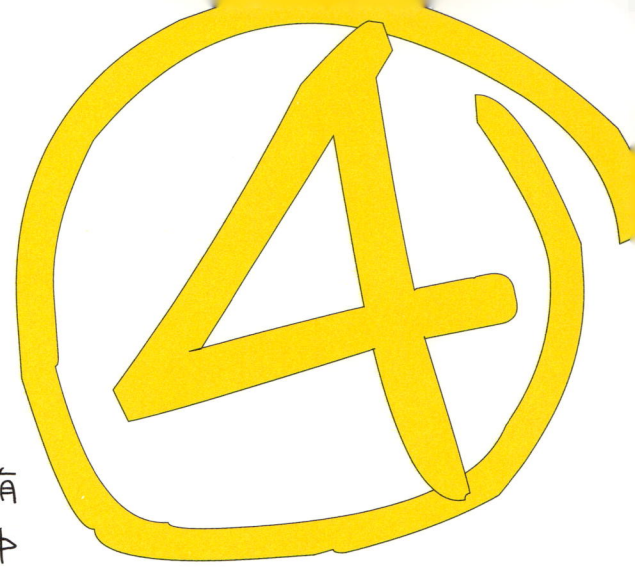

Q：外滩边上的江是什么江呢？

外滩在上海市黄浦区的黄浦江边上，所以也叫黄浦滩。外滩全长有1.5公里，长长的马路边矗立着52幢风格迥异的古典复兴大楼，是中国近现代重要史迹及代表性建筑。同时外滩也是第四批全国重点文物保护单位哦。

开放时间：全天

Q: Do you know the name of the river by the Bund?

The Bund lies by Huangpu River in Huangpu district, Shanghai; therefore, it is also called 'Huangpu Riverside'. It stretches for 1.5 kilometers, along which 52 classically revival buildings of distinguished styles stand. They are important historical and typical architectures of modern China. Meanwhile the Bund is among the fourth batch of national key cultural relics protection units.

Opening hours: All day

新天地 Xintiandi

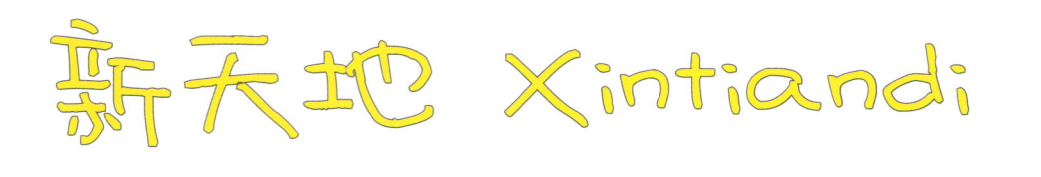

⑤

Q：新天地的房子改建自什么风格的建筑呢？

上海新天地的房子参考了石库门的风格，在改变了石库门原有的居住功能同时，添加了商业经营功能，把这片反映了上海历史和文化的老房子改造成有餐饮、购物、演艺等多种功能的时尚、休闲、文化一体化的娱乐中心。

开放时间：全天

Q: What kind of architecture has Xintiandi been remodeled from?

The buildings in Xintiandi referred to the style of Shikumen. Those original residences have been transformed into commercial places, marking the turning of old buildings inscribed with the history and culture of Shanghai into a leisure center featuring dining, shopping and performing arts.

Opening hours: All day

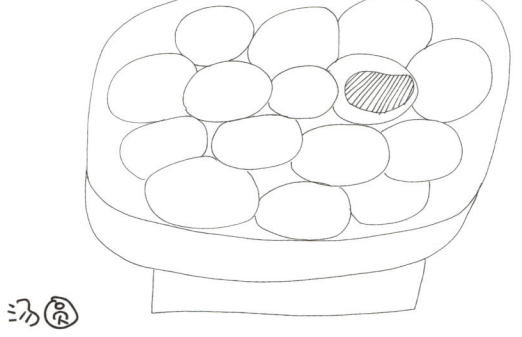

汤圆
Sweet Dumplings

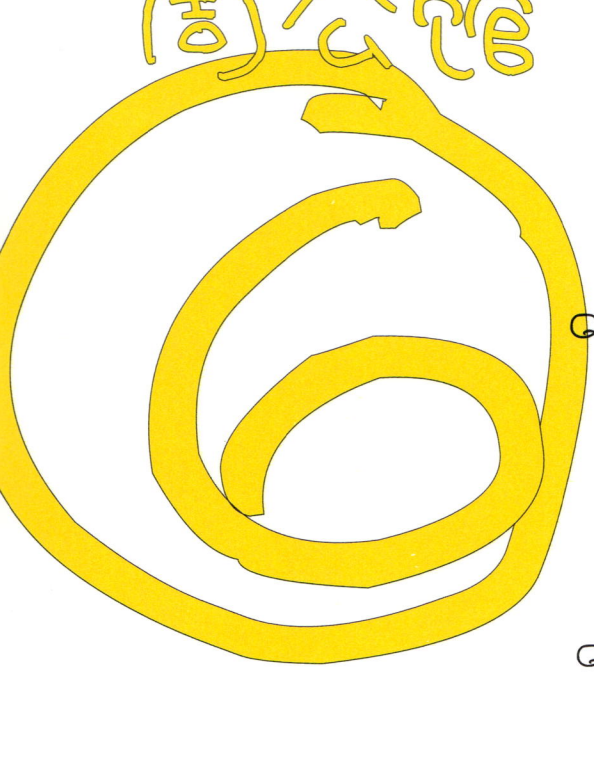

Former Residence of ZHOU Enlai

Q：小朋友们知道当年是哪一位领导人居住在这里吗？

周公馆位于著名的思南路上。在1946年-1947年中国国民党与中国共产党谈判期间，周恩来在这里工作和生活，还接待过美国总统特使马歇尔。到了1979年的时候，周公馆恢复了原貌，变身成为纪念馆。

开放时间：9:00-16:30（最晚16:00进场）

Q: Do you know how many years Soong Ching Ling spent here?
Former Residence of ZHOU Enlai is located on the famous Sinan Road. During the negotiations between Chinese KMT(Kuo Min Tang) and CCP(Chinese Communist Party) from 1946 to 1947, Mr. ZHOU Enlai lived and worked here, and received U.S. Presidential Envoy Marshall. By the time of 1979, this residence was restored into original state then turned into a memorial hall.
Opening hours: 9:00-16:30 (last entry 16:00)

上海宋庆龄故居纪念馆
Soong Ching Ling Memorial Residence in Shanghai

Q：小朋友们知道宋庆龄奶奶在这里居住了多久吗？

中华人民共和国名誉主席宋庆龄奶奶曾经居住过的大房子，是在清朝康熙年间造好的，历史很悠久了呢。院子里有30多株宋奶奶最喜欢的香樟树，她曾经在这里生活和工作了15年，直到逝世。现在宋庆龄故居还是全国重点文物保护单位。

开放时间：周二 - 周日 9:00-16:30（周一闭馆，节假日除外）

Q: Do you know how many years Soong Ching Ling spent here?
This big house, where the honorary Chairman of China, Song Ching Ling used to live, was built during the reign of Kangxi, Qing dynasty. It has witnessed a lot of history. Over 30 camphor trees were planted here, that is Mrs. Soong's favorite tree. She had spent her life and work time here for 15 years until she passed away. Now the former residence is a national key cultural relics protection unit.
Opening hours: Tue. - Sun. 9:00-16:30 (Closed on Mondays, holidays excluded)

陆家嘴 Lujiazui

Q：中国第一高楼是哪一栋建筑？

陆家嘴位于浦东新区的黄浦江畔，隔江面对外滩，是中国最具影响力的金融中心之一。

上海环球金融中心楼高492米，一共有101层。

开放时间：9:00-21:30（进场）

金茂大厦楼高420.5米，加上顶端尖塔共有93层。

开放时间：8:30-21:30

上海中心大厦楼高632米，竣工时是中国第一及世界第二高楼！

开放时间：8:30-21:30（进场）

东方明珠广播电视塔，塔高约468米，承担着上海6套无线电视发射任务。里面还有太空舱、旋转餐厅等好玩的地方哦！

开放时间：8:00-21:30

Q: Which building is the tallest one in China?

Located on the bank of the Huangpu River in Pudong New Area, Lujiazui faces the Bund across the river and is one of the most influential financial centers in China.

Shanghai Global Financial Center is 492 meters high, with 101 floors in total.

Opening hours: 9:00-22:30 (last entry at 21:30)

Jinmao Tower is 420.5 meters high, with 93 floors counting the spire on top!

Opening hours: 8:30-21:30

Shanghai Tower is 632 meters high. It once was the tallest building in China and the second tallest building in the world when topped out.

Opening hours: 8:30-22:00 (last entry at 21:30)

Oriental Pearl TV Tower about 468 meters high and in charge of six sets of radio and television transmission services. Aside from transmitting signals, it also features attractions such as space capsule and revolving restaurant.

Opening hours: 8:00-21:30

上海迪士尼度假区
shanghai Disney Resort

Q：上海迪士尼是全球第几个迪士尼度假区？听到迪士尼有没有很开心？

上海迪士尼度假区在2016年6月16日开园，是中国大陆第一座迪士尼度假区，也是全球第六个迪士尼度假区。

开放时间：8:00-22:00

Q: How many Disney Resorts are there worldwide now? How do you feel on hearing 'Disneyland'? Excited?

Opened on June 16, 2016, Shanghai Disney Resort is the first Resort in mainland China and sixth Disney Resort in the world.

Opening hours: 8:00-22:00

上海野生动物园
Shanghai Wild ⑩ Animal Park

Q：为什么在上海野生动物园内，人是被关在车厢里的？

上海野生动物园是中国首座国家级野生动物园，在1995年11月18日正式对外开放，动物园大到可以玩一整天哦。现在动物园还升级成了国家5A级旅游区，里面有着200多种珍稀野生动物，在猛兽区的范围内是一定要坐在有栏杆的车里参观的。

开放时间：3月-11月8:00-17:00；7月-8月8:00-18:00；12月-次年2月8:30-16:30

Q: What kind of architecture has Xintiandi been remodeled from?
Being China's first national-level wildlife park, Shanghai Wildlife Park was officially opened to public on November 18th, 1995. It is recommended to spend a whole day exploring the grand zoo. Now the zoo has been upgraded to a national 5A-level tourist destination with more than 200 rare wild animals. When visiting beast area, riding in a car with railing is a MUST!
Opening hours: Mar.-Nov. 8:00-17:00; Jul.-Aug. 8:00-18:00; Dec.-Feb. 8:30-16:30

朱家角古镇
Zhujiajiao
Ancient Town

豆浆油条
Soybean Milk and Fried Bread Stick

Q：朱家角古镇中最大的桥叫什么名字？

朱家角内最大的桥叫放生桥。以前每逢农历初一都是放生日期，并且还是禁止渔人捕捞打鱼的日子。朱家角既是上海四大历史文化名镇之一、中国第一批特色小镇，也是全国最美特色小城镇50强。

开放时间：全天

Q: What's the name of the largest bridge in Zhujiajiao Watertown?
The largest bridge in Zhujiajiao Ancient Town is called Fangsheng Qiao, namely, bridge to free captive animals. People used to free fish on the first day of lunar calendar and fishmen were forbidden to fish on the same day. Being a town with memorable characters, Zhujiajiao is not only one of the four renowned historic and cultural towns in Shanghai, but also among the top 50 most beautiful towns in China.
Opening hours: All day

东平国家森林公园
Dongping National Forest Park

Q：小朋友们知道东平国家森林公园在哪个岛上吗？

东平国家森林公园在上海市崇明岛上哦，总面积有3.55平方公里，大概有560个足球场那么大！公园里80%以上都是森林，植物资源非常丰富。东平国家森林公园还是国家级的哦！很酷吧。

开放时间：周一 — 周五 8:00-16:00，周六 — 周日 8:30-17:00

Q: Hey, do you know which island Dongping National Forest Park is on?
Dongping National Forest Park is on Chongming Island in Shanghai. Its total area is 3.55 square kilometers, which is about 560 football fields! More than 80% of the park is covered by forests, and the plant resources are so rich. Plus, it is one of the national parks in China. Isn't it cool?
Opening hours: Mon.-Fri. 8:00-16:00, Sat.-Sun. 8:30-17:00

图书在版编目（CIP）数据

这里是上海：汉英对照 / 黄瑶瑶绘. — 北京：中
国城市出版社, 2019.9
（阿姬的涂色旅行）
ISBN 978-7-5074-3199-5

Ⅰ. ①这… Ⅱ. ①黄… Ⅲ. ①旅游指南－上海－儿童
读物－汉、英②绘画技法－儿童读物－汉、英 Ⅳ.
①K928.951-49②J21-49

中国版本图书馆 CIP 数据核字 (2019) 第 192455 号

责任编辑：徐明怡
策划：那行童书
责任校对：王烨 党蕾
装帧设计：七月合作社

阿姬的涂色旅行
这里是上海
黄瑶瑶 绘
*
中国城市出版社 出版、发行（北京海淀三里河路 9 号）
各地新华书店、建筑书店经销
上海雅昌艺术印制有限公司 制版、印制
*
开本：787×1092 毫米 横 1/16 印张：1¾ 字数：4 千字
2019 年 10 月第一版 2019 年 10 月第一次印刷
定价：38.00 元
ISBN 978-7-5074-3199-5
（904182）

版权所有 翻印必究
如有印装质量问题，可寄本社退换
（邮政编码 100037）

黄瑶瑶 Huang Yaoyao

80 后留日插画师
东京多摩美术大学插画研究生
师从日本最著名的插画师秋山孝教授
留日期间作品在多摩大学、秋山美术馆、青山 gallery5610 馆等展出，
学成归国后首创系列绘本《今天要去哪里》，热销中

2018 上海国际少儿生活方式展 特邀装置创作人
2017 SUSAS 上海城市空间艺术季 诚邀艺术家
《乐享浦江——两岸贯通公共空间导览地图册》 插画师
《SUSAS Mook》2018 年 10 月创刊首期 插画师
中国城市出版社城市涂色刊物 插画师

策划 / 出品：**那行 NEXTMIXING**